The Best Christmas Coloring Book:

Coloring Books for Kids & Children

Copyright © 2019 by kpublisher

kPublisher

This book belongs to:

....

....

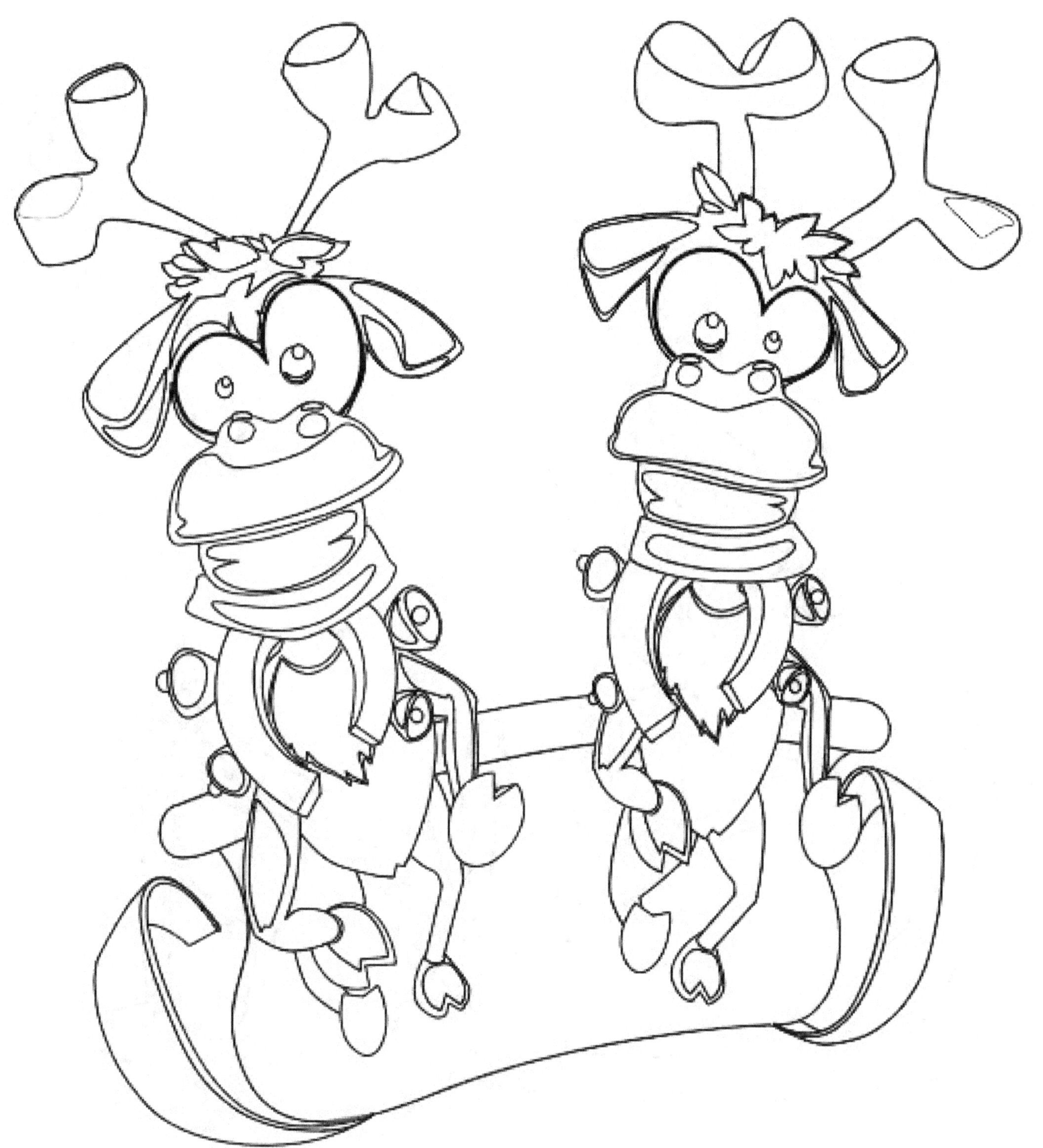

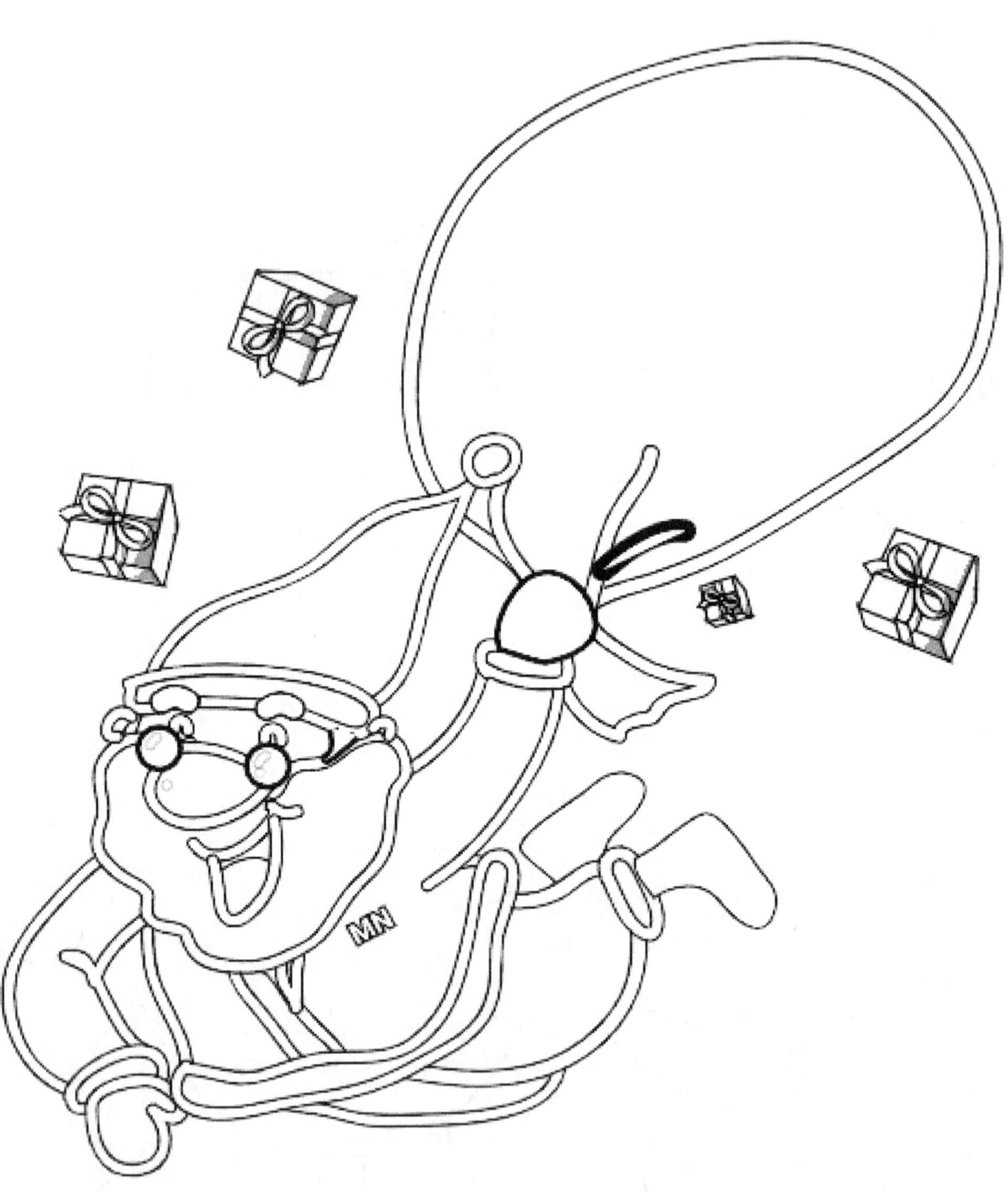

Merry Christmas

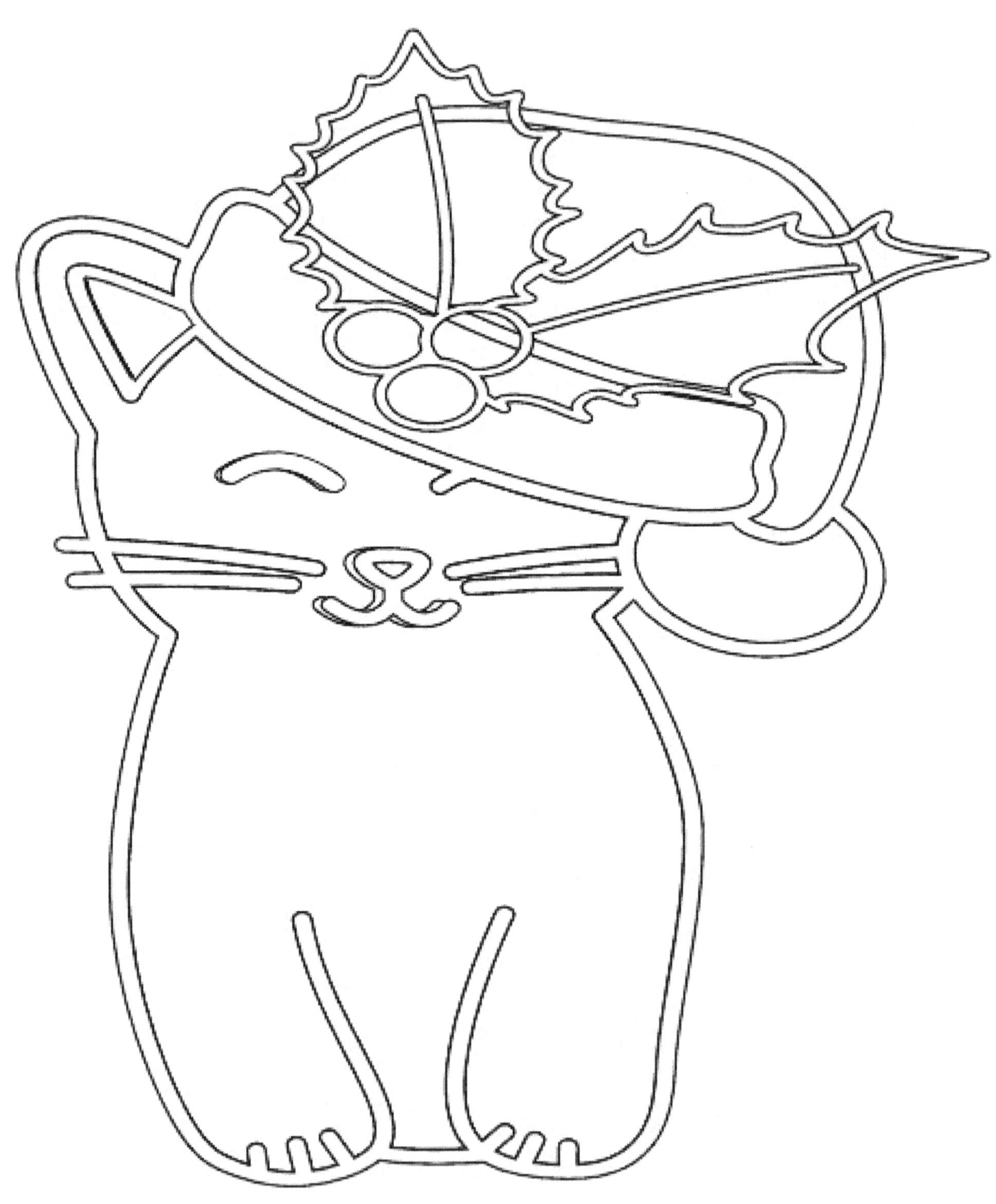

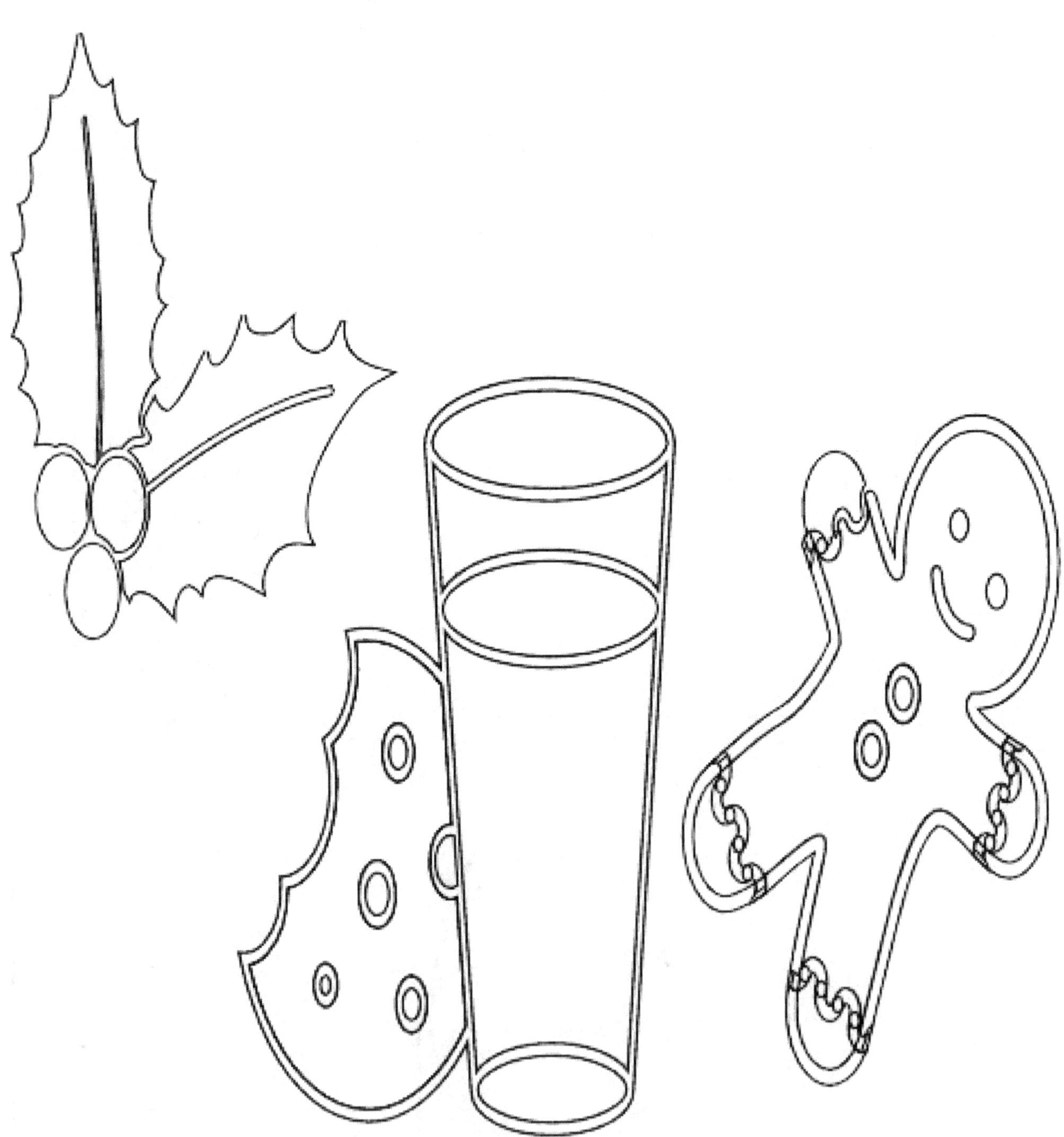

God Bless Us
Everyone

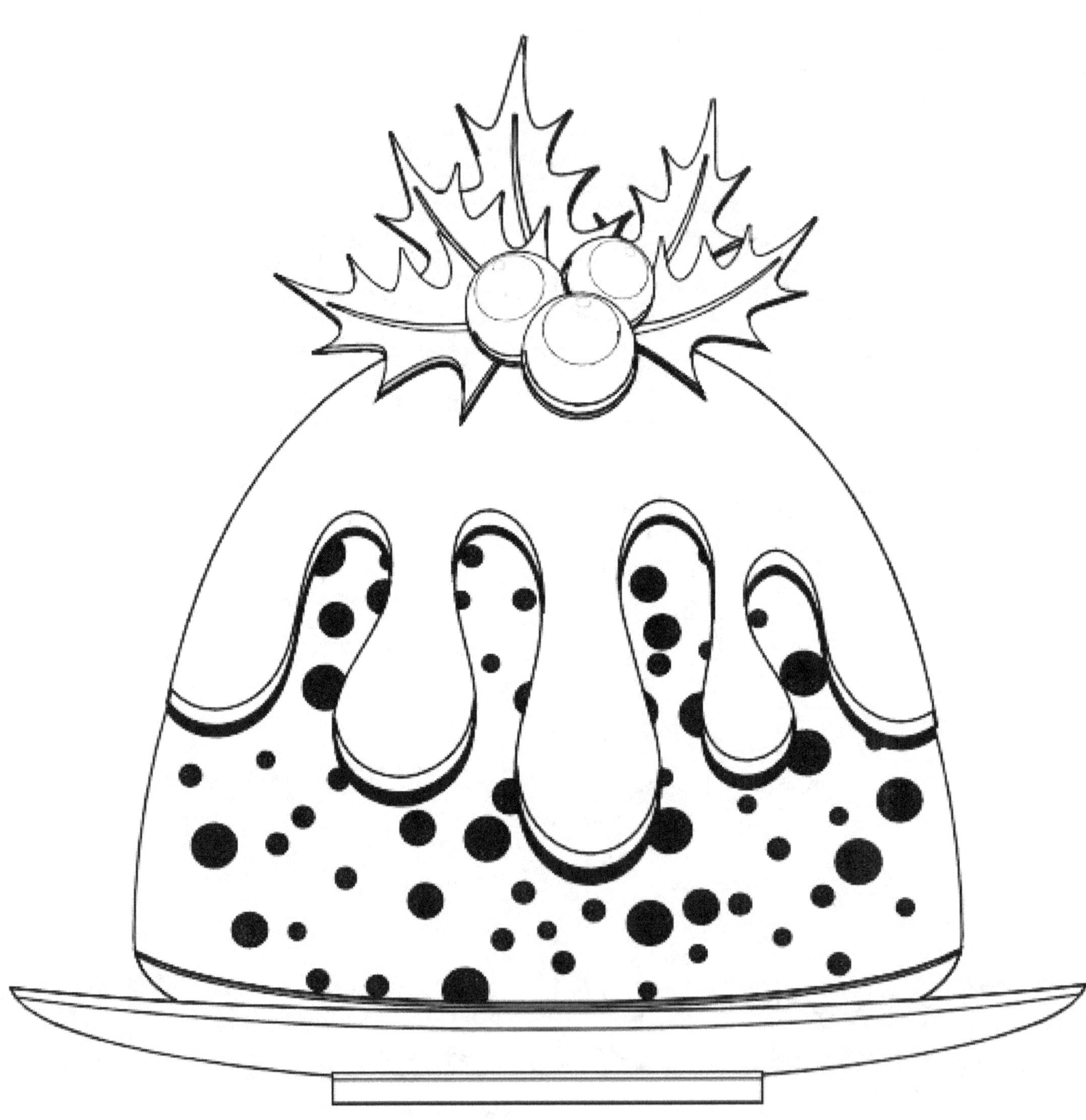

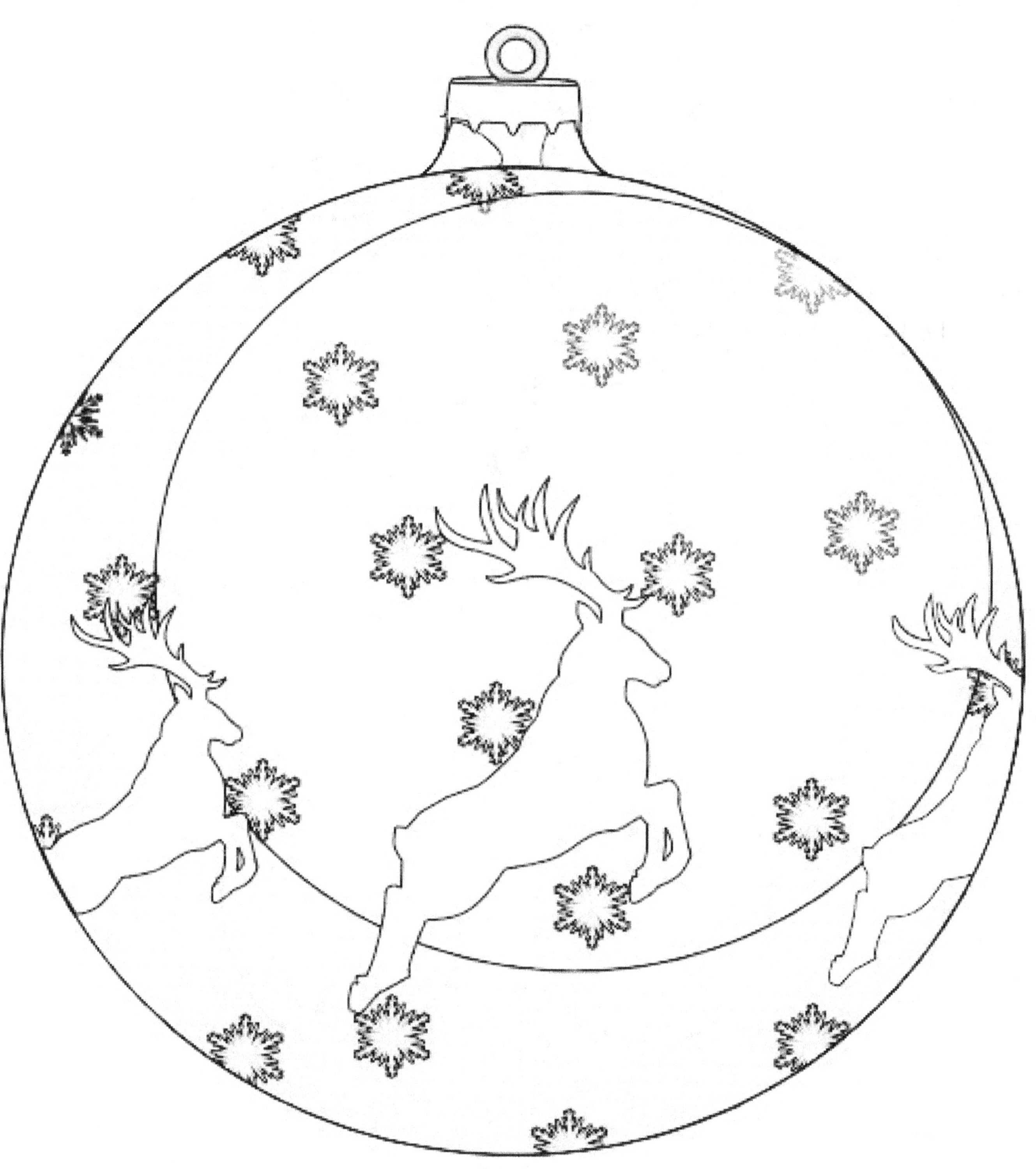

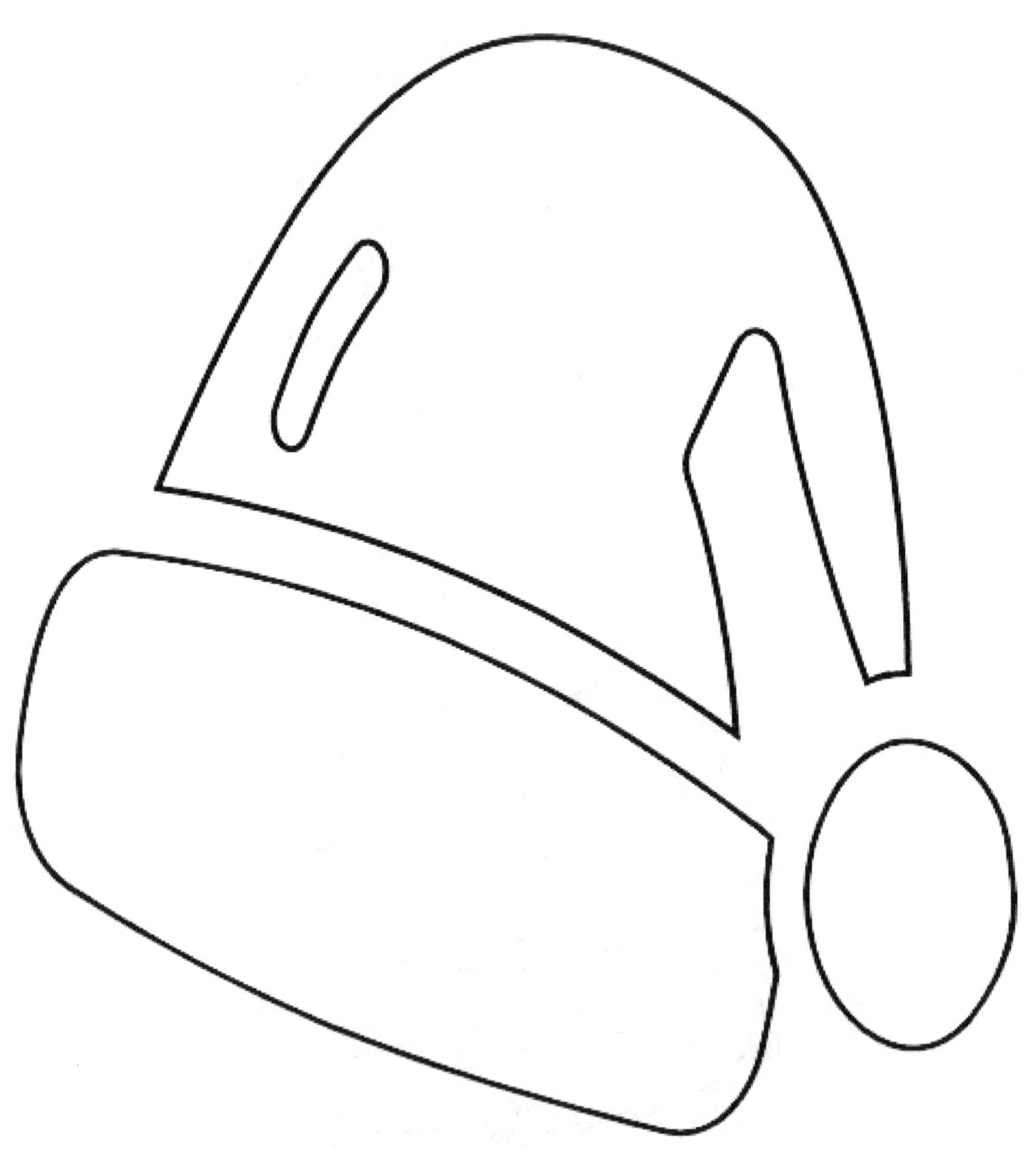

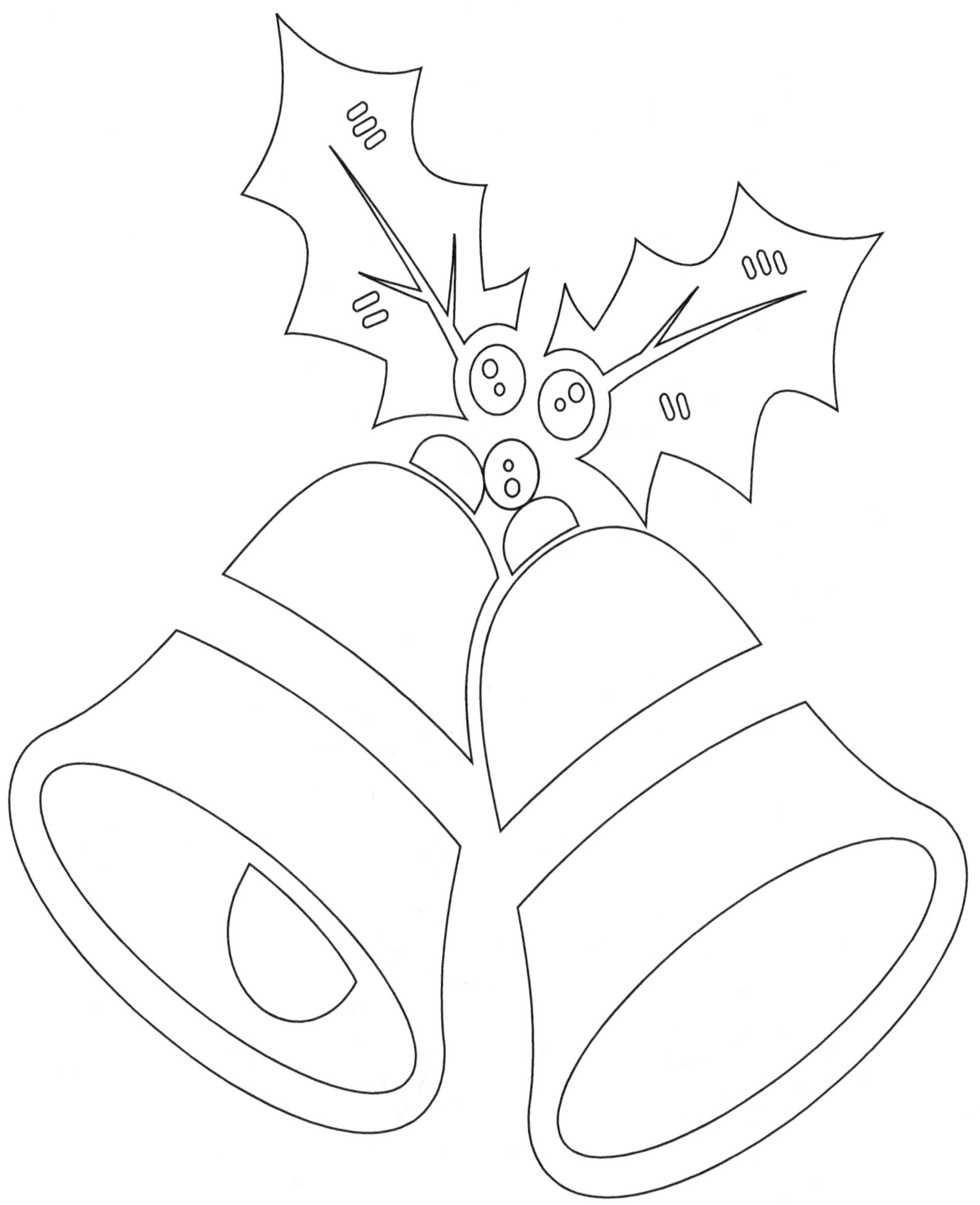

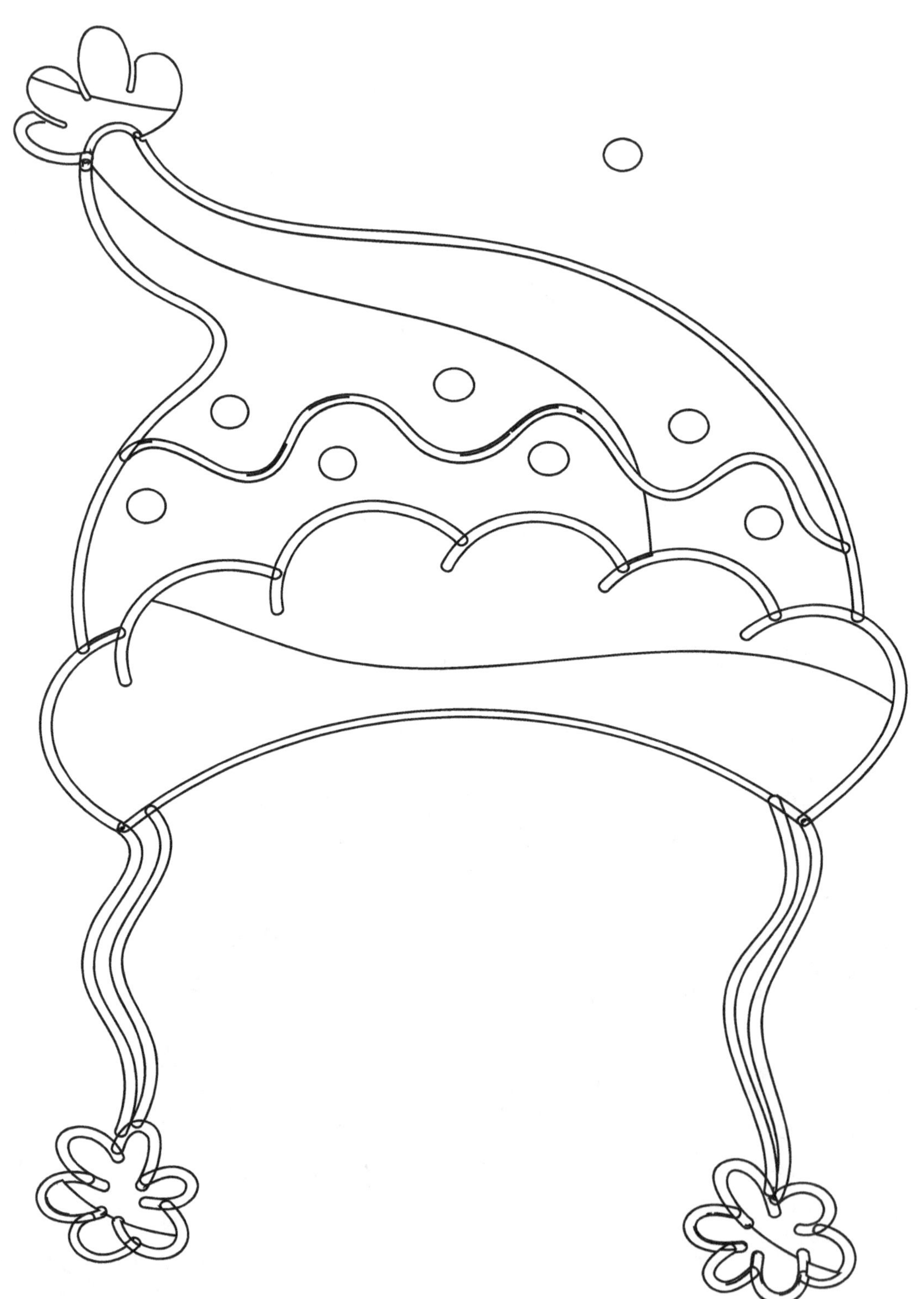

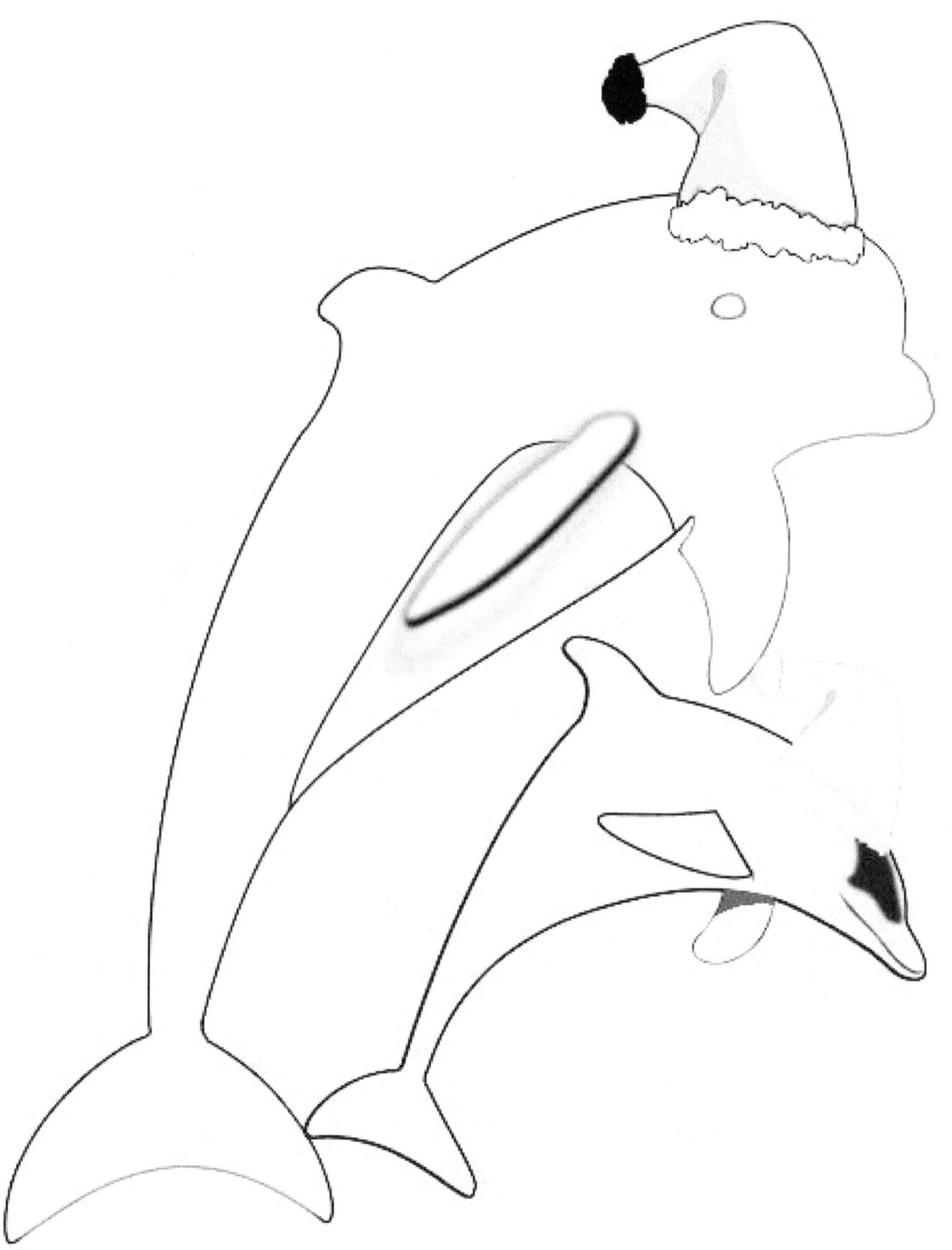

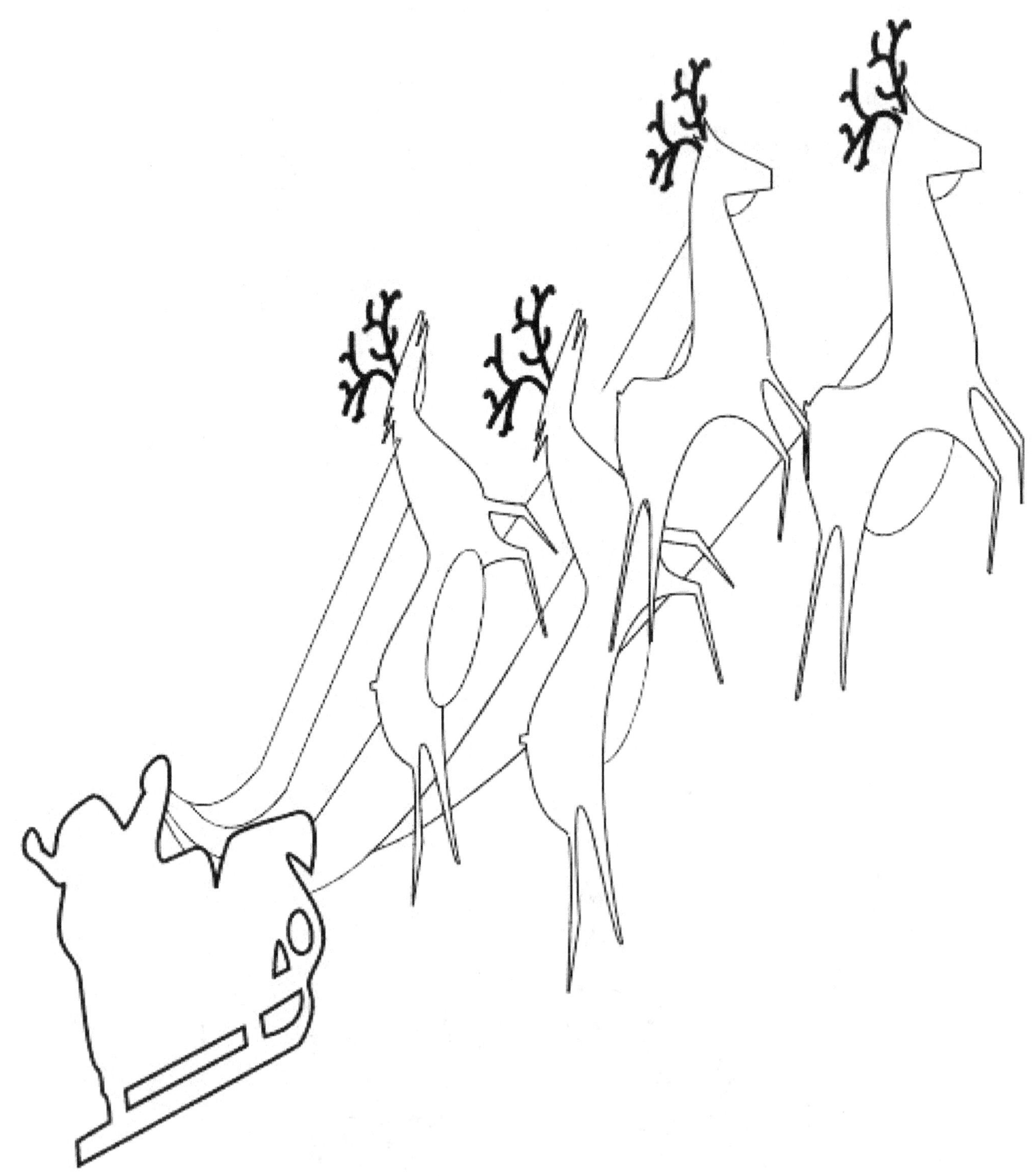

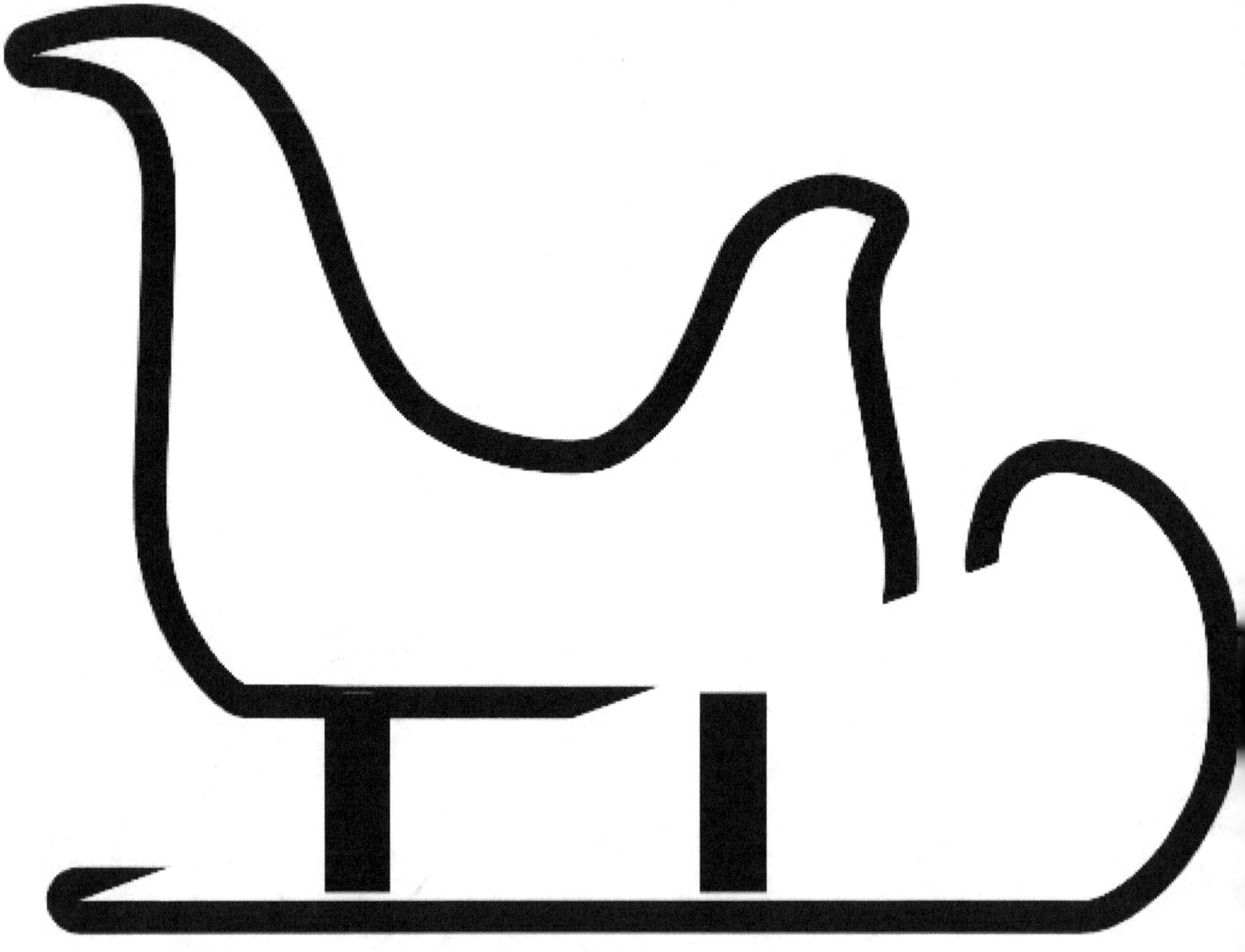

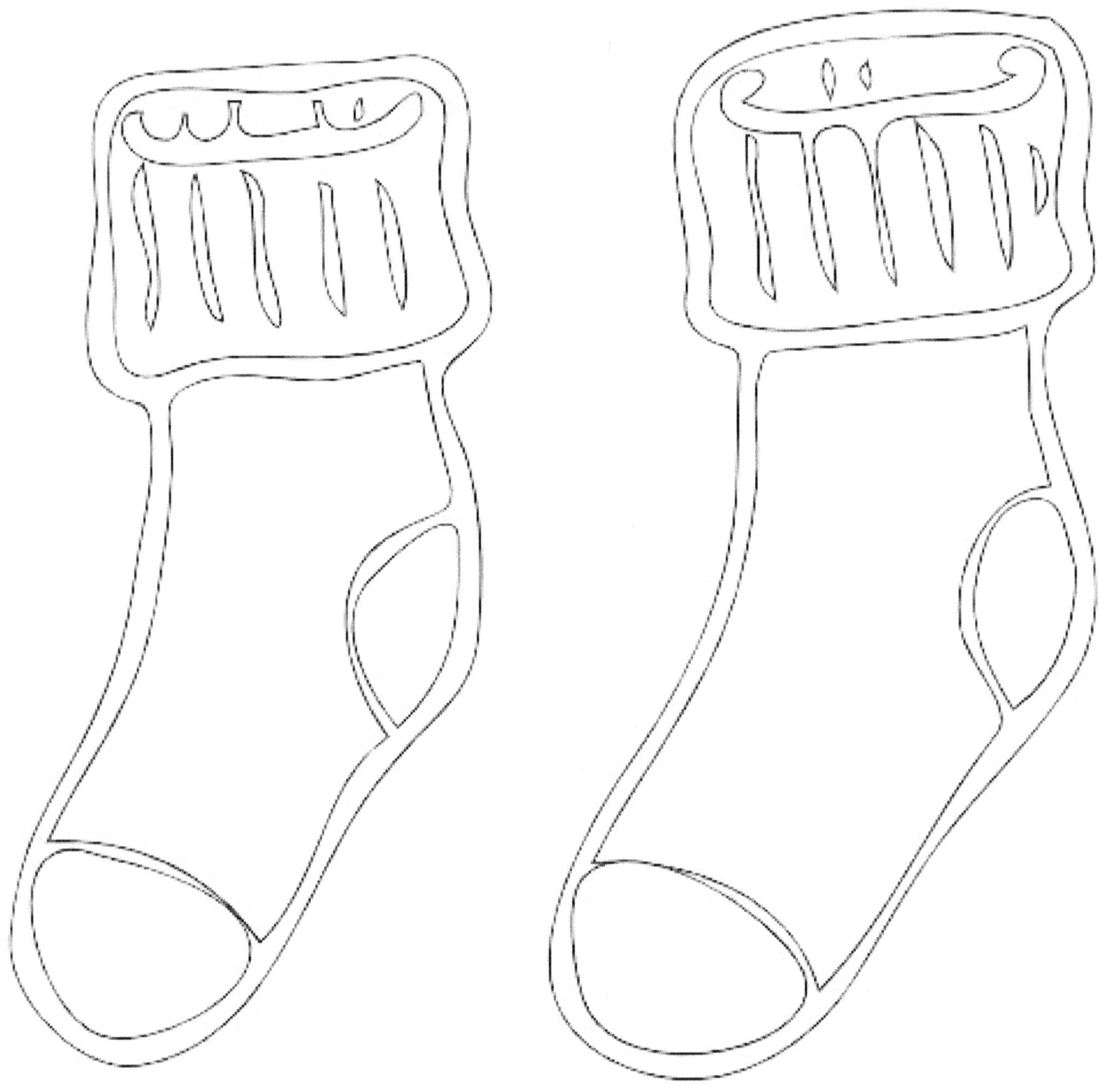

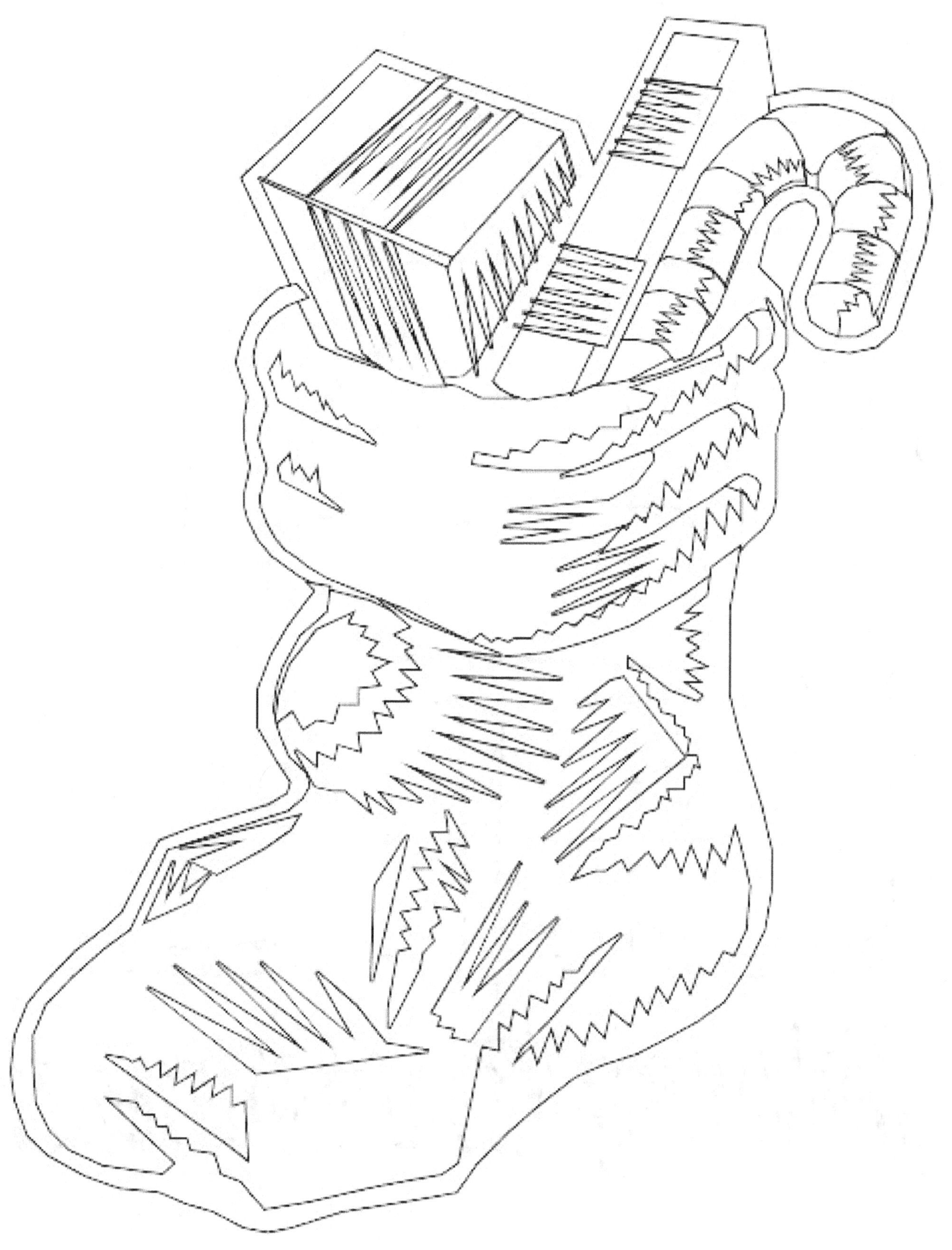

Merry Christmas

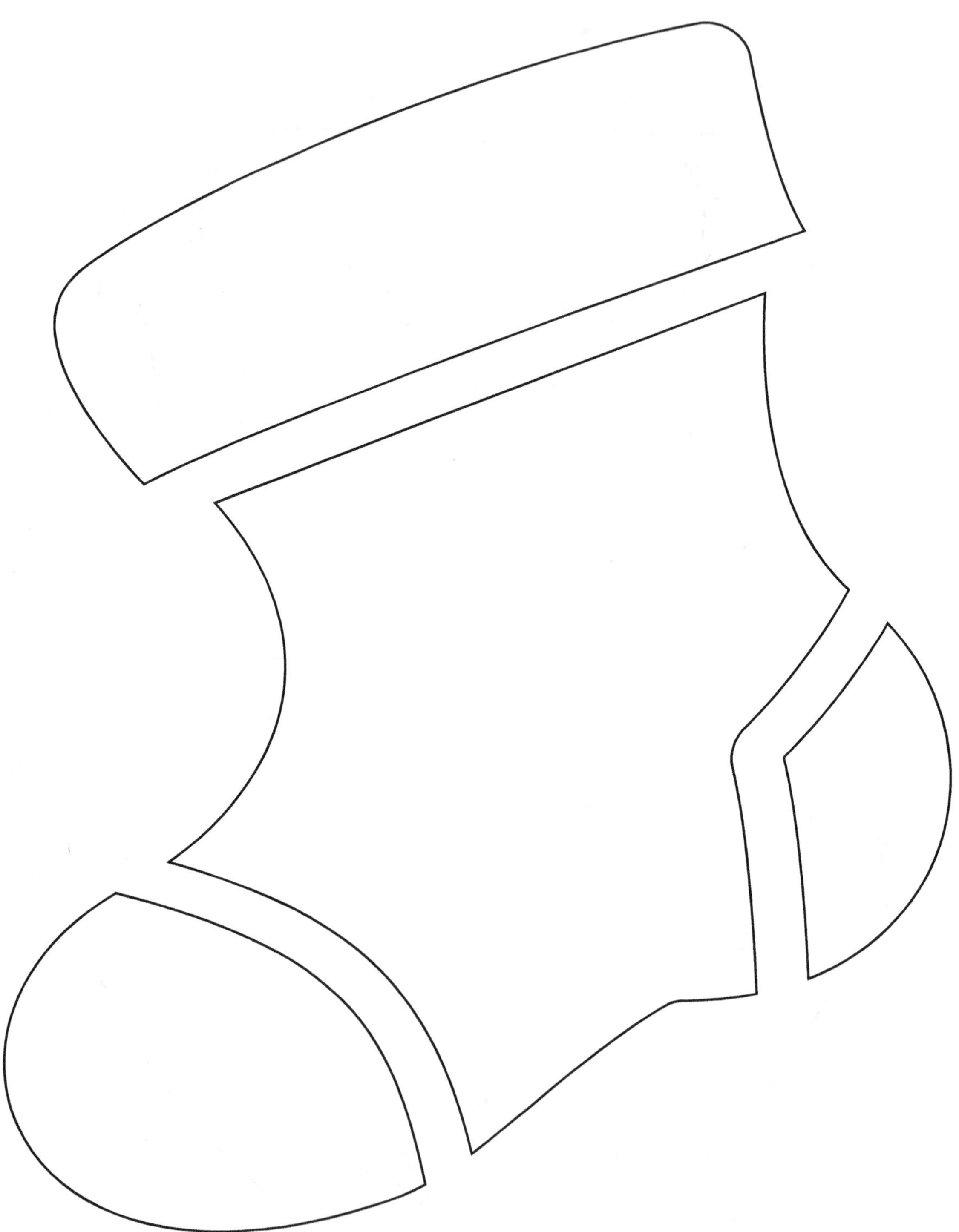

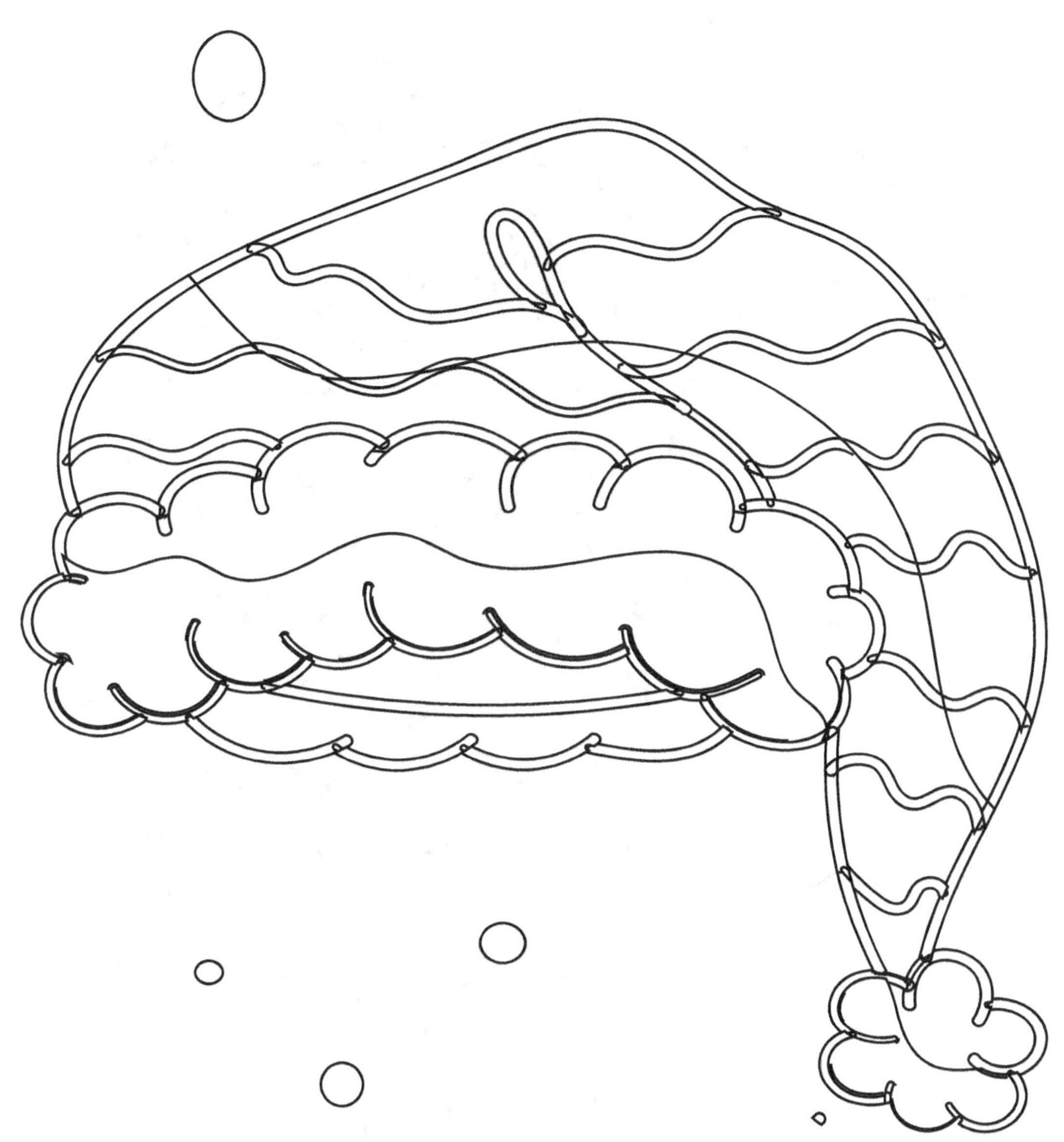

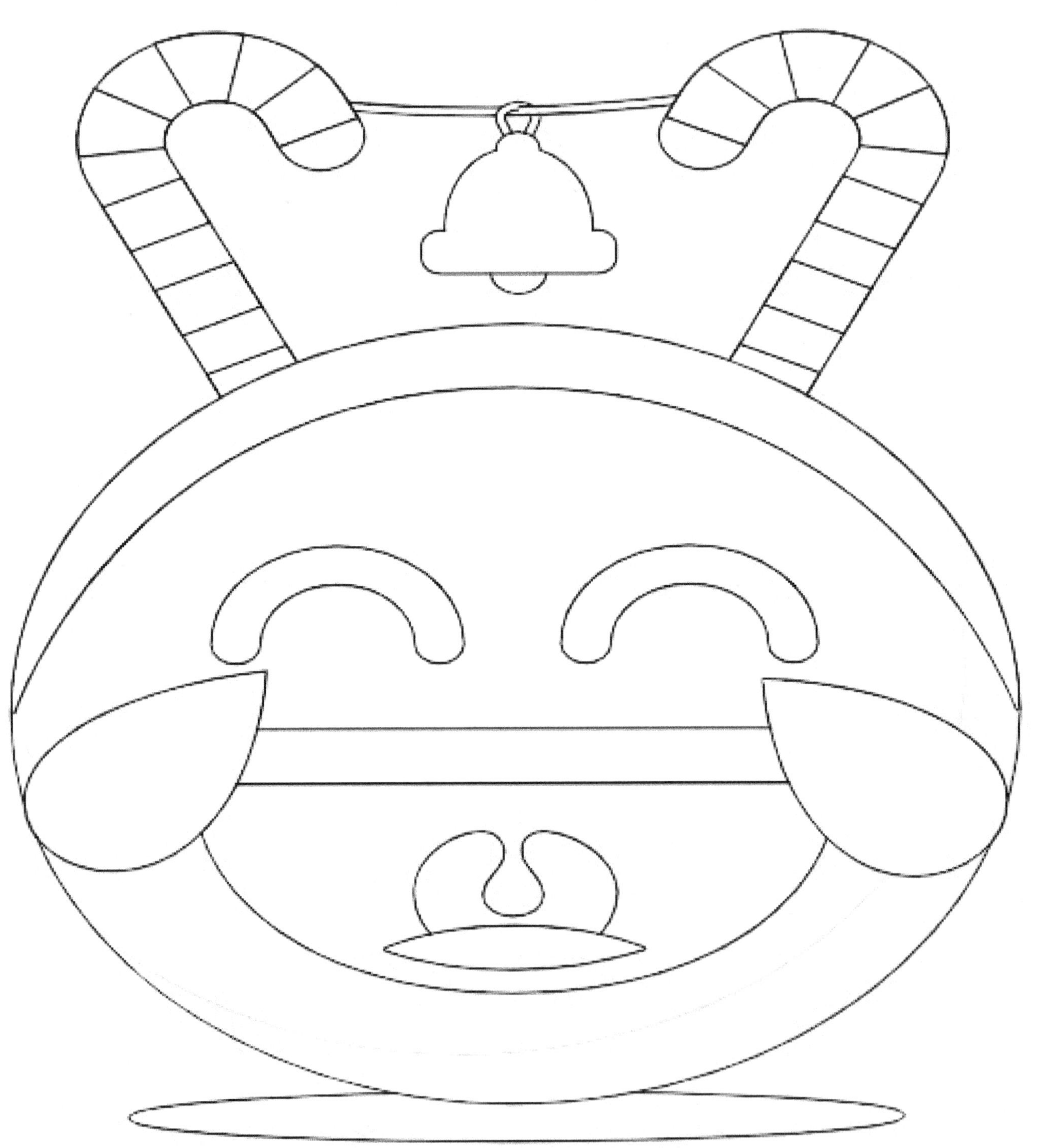

www.ingramcontent.com/pod-product-compliance
Lightning Source LLC
Chambersburg PA
CBHW081436250726
48662CB00009B/2822